Wonders

McGraw Hill Education

Cover and Title Page: Nathan Love

www.mheonline.com/readingwonders

Send all inquiries to:
McGraw-Hill Education
2 Penn Plaza
New York, NY 10121

ISBN: 978-0-02-130618-3
MHID: 0-02-130618-4

Printed in the United States of America.

11 12 13 MER 27 26 25   D

Wonders

ELD
Companion Worktext

Program Authors

Diane August

Jana Echevarria

Josefina V. Tinajero

McGraw Hill Education

Unit 2

Taking the Next Step

Taking the
Next
Step

The Big Idea

What does it take to put a plan into action?

3

4

What do you see on the flag? Based on the picture, what did George Washington and Betsy Ross do to make a new flag? Describe what people do to solve problems.

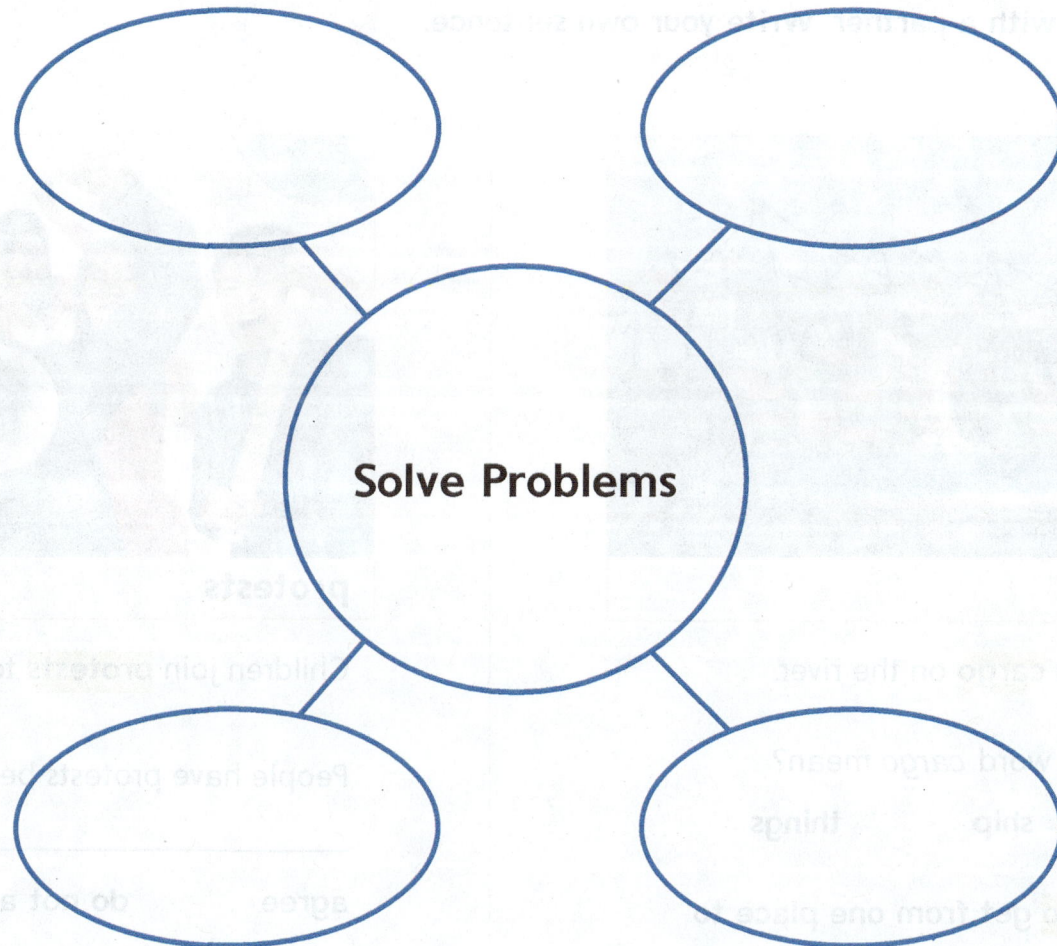

Solve Problems

Discuss what people do to solve problems. Use the words from the chart. You can say:

People can _____

to solve a problem.

More Vocabulary

Look at the picture. Read the word. Then read the sentence. Talk about the word with a partner. Write your own sentence.

cargo

The ship carries **cargo** on the river.

What does the word *cargo* mean?

water   **ship**   **things**

How does cargo get from one place to another?

Cargo travels on a _____.

protests

Children join **protests** to protect the earth.

People have protests because they _____

_____ with something.

agree   **do not agree**

Have you seen or heard about a protest?

People _____

_____

at a protest.

Fancy Collection/SuperStock; ranplett/E+/Getty Images

Words and Phrases: *except* and *instead*

The word *except* means "not including."

Are all the chairs purple?

No, all the chairs are purple **except** the yellow chair.

The word *instead* means "in the place of."

Which shirt does Tyler want?

Tyler wants the blue shirt **instead** of the plaid shirt.

Talk with a partner. Look at the pictures. Read the sentences. Write the word that completes each sentence.

COLLABORATE

Macy can eat an apple or she can eat a banana _____.

      except   **instead**

Everyone is wearing a red cap _____ _____ Michio.

      except   **instead**

COLLABORATE

1 Talk About It

Look at the picture. Read the title. Talk about what you see. Use these words.

document signing colonists date Congress independence

Write about what you see.

I see _____

_____.

The document shows _____

_____.

The man is _____

a _____.

The colonists want _____

_____.

Take notes as you read the text.

Creating a Nation

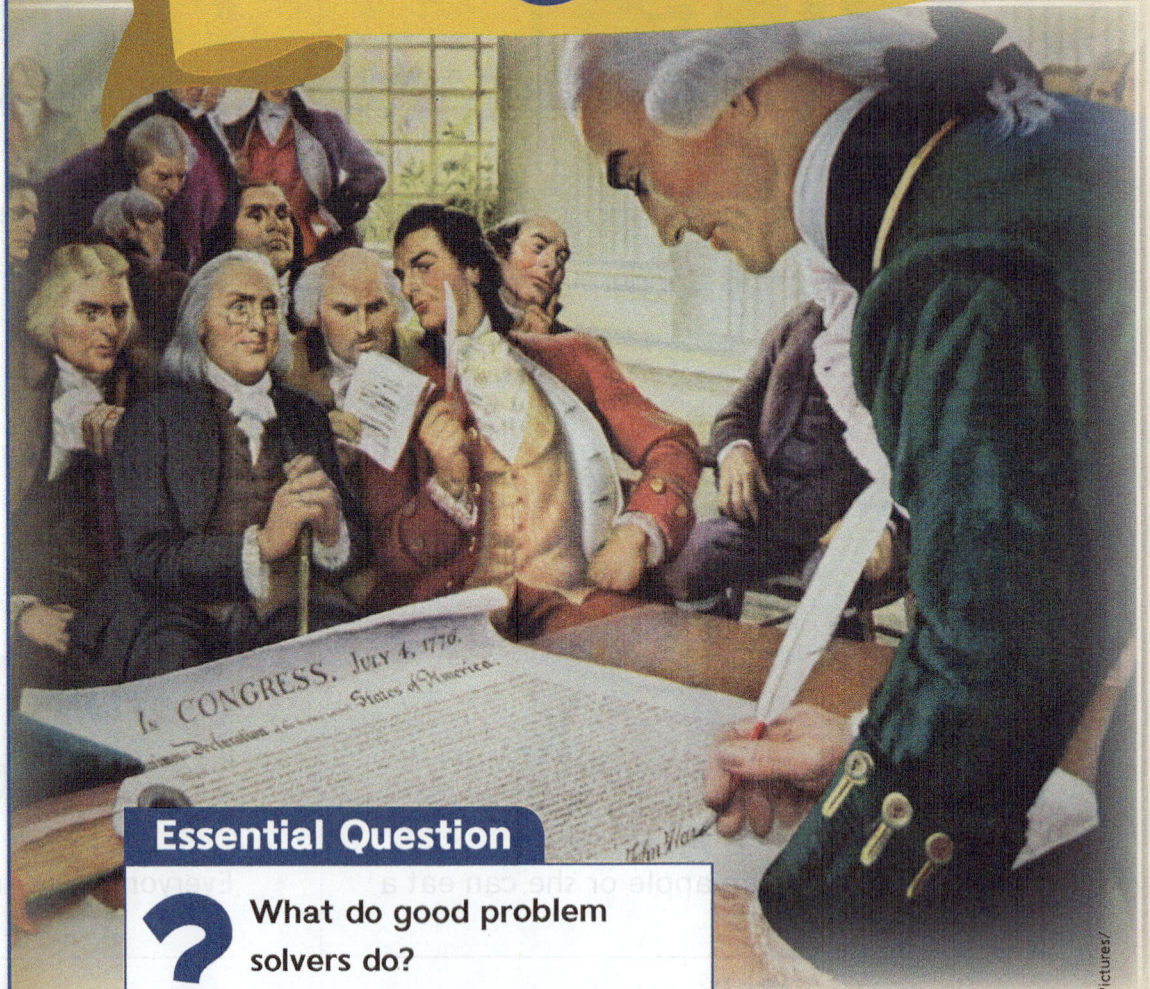

To CONGRESS, JULY 4, 1776.
States of America.

Essential Question

?

What do good problem solvers do?

Read about how American colonists solved their problems with Great Britain.

Taxes and Protests

In 1765, King George III of Great Britain needed money to rule an empire. He decided to raise taxes. As a result, the British government passed a new tax called the Stamp Act. So when colonists bought any type of paper, the paper had a stamp. Then the colonists had to pay a tax on the stamp!

Most colonists thought the Stamp Act was unfair. They did not have representatives to vote or make decisions for them in the British government. The colonists did not want to pay the tax because they didn't vote for it.

The colonists had protests against the Stamp Act. As a result, the act was canceled, but the government put taxes on other things. Then in 1770, in Boston,

Boston Tea Party: Some colonists wore costumes to look like Native Americans.

British soldiers shot into an angry crowd and killed five colonists. This tragedy is known as the Boston Massacre.

By 1773, most taxes were repealed, or canceled, except the tax on tea. One night, the colonists in Boston boarded three British ships and tossed a cargo of tea into the water to protest the tax on tea. This event is called the Boston Tea Party.

Anonymous/Getty Images; (bkgd) Oleksiy Maksymenko/Alamy

Text Evidence

1 Comprehension
Problem and Solution

Reread the first paragraph. What problem did King George have? Underline the problem. What is the solution? Put a box around the text.

2 Specific Vocabulary Ⓐ Ⓒ Ⓣ

The word *unfair* has the prefix *un-* and means "not right or just." What was unfair? Put a box around the text. Why did the colonists think this way? Circle the text.

3 Sentence Structure Ⓐ Ⓒ Ⓣ

Reread the second sentence in the second paragraph. Who did not have representatives? Underline the text. What do representatives do? Circle the text. Write about it.

Representatives _____

_____

for colonists.

Text Evidence

1 Specific Vocabulary A C T

The word *undecided* has the prefix *un-* and means "not decided." What were the colonists undecided about? Circle the text. What does the prefix *un-* mean? Use meanings of *unfair* and *undecided* as clues.

The meaning of the prefix *un-* is

_____.

2 Comprehension
Problem and Solution

Reread the first and second paragraphs. What problem did the First Continental Congress try to solve? Underline the text.

The problem was the colonists

_____.

COLLABORATE

3 Talk About It

Why did the colonists meet for the Second Continental Congress? Use text evidence to support your answer.

American Revolution Begins

The Boston Tea Party angered King George. He closed the Boston port and banned town meetings to punish the colonists. Consequently, some colonists wanted independence from Britain. Other colonists wanted peace with the king. Many colonists were undecided.

Finally, representatives from each colony met to decide what to do. This important meeting was the First Continental Congress. It took place in Philadelphia in 1774. The representatives decided to send a peace proposal to the king, but this did not solve the problem.

In April 1775, British troops marched to Lexington and Concord. These villages were near Boston. Militias met the British troops. Militias were groups of colonists who were ready to fight. The British troops attacked, so the militias fought back. The American Revolution began.

The colonists met for a Second Continental Congress in May to organize for the war. The members of the Congress voted George Washington to be the commander of a new army. The representatives also chose Thomas Jefferson to write a declaration of independence.

Events of the American Revolution

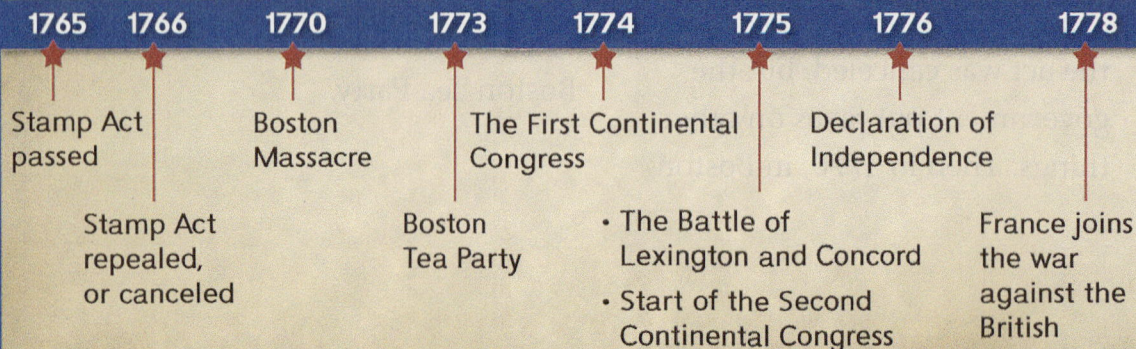

1765	1766	1770	1773	1774	1775	1776	1778
Stamp Act passed		Boston Massacre		The First Continental Congress		Declaration of Independence	
	Stamp Act repealed, or canceled		Boston Tea Party	• The Battle of Lexington and Concord • Start of the Second Continental Congress			France joins the war against the British

Independence

Jefferson needed to convince the colonists that they needed independence from Britain. Jefferson explained that people have rights to life, liberty, and the pursuit of happiness. And, the government needs to protect these rights. Instead, King George took away the rights. Therefore, the colonies needed independence from Britain.

Congress debated Jefferson's arguments. On July 4, 1776, Congress approved the Declaration of Independence. A nation was born.

In 1778, France helped the colonists fight Britain. Then in 1781, the British surrendered. That year Congress approved a plan for a new government called the Articles of Confederation. The plan gave more power to the states than a central government.

The war was over, but the United States government was not working well. The states disagreed with one another. In 1787, work on a new plan began at the Constitutional Convention.

(bkgd) Oleksiy Maksymenko/Alamy

1781	1783
• Last major battle of the War	King George recognizes independence of United States
• The Articles of Confederation approved	

Make Connections

? Talk about how American colonists tried to solve their problems with Great Britain. **ESSENTIAL QUESTION**

Think of a time you had a problem. How did you solve the problem? **TEXT TO SELF**

1 **Specific Vocabulary** Ⓐ Ⓒ Ⓣ

The word *rights* means "something a person has or can do by law." What rights do people have? Underline the text. What other rights do people have?

People have the rights to _____

_____.

2 **Sentence Structure** Ⓐ Ⓒ Ⓣ

Reread the third sentence of the third paragraph. What does the phrase *That year* refer to? Circle the text that tells you. What happened in 1781?

In 1781, _____

and _____.

COLLABORATE

3 **Talk About It**

Reread the last paragraph. What was the purpose of the Constitutional Convention?

The purpose was to _____

_____.

Respond to the Text

COLLABORATE **Partner Discussion** Work with a partner. Read the questions about "Creating a Nation." Show where you found text evidence. Write the page numbers. Then discuss what you learned.

What problem did the colonists have?

I read that the British government passed a _____

_____

Page(s): _____

The colonists thought the Stamp Act was _____ because

_____.

Page(s): _____

Text Evidence 🔍

How did the colonists try to solve the problem?

At the First Continental Congress, the colonists decided to _____

_____.

Page(s): _____

At the Second Continental Congress, the colonists decided to _____

_____.

Page(s): _____

Text Evidence 🔍

COLLABORATE **Group Discussion** Present your answers to the group. Cite text evidence for your ideas. Listen to and discuss the group's opinions.

Write Work with a partner. Look at your notes about "Creating a Nation."
Write your answer to the Essential Question. Use text evidence to support your
answer. Use vocabulary words in your writing.

COLLABORATE

How did the colonists solve their problem?

The colonists wanted independence from _____

because _____.

To solve the problem, the colonists met and decided to _____

_____

_____.

The colonists were good problem solvers because _____

_____.

Share Writing Present your writing to the class. Discuss their opinions.
Talk about their ideas. Explain why you agree or disagree with their ideas.
You can say:

I agree that _____.

I do not agree because _____.

Write to Sources

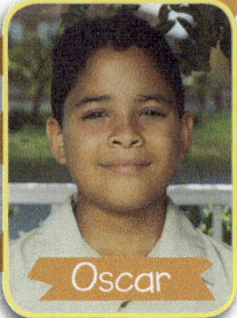

Take Notes About the Text I took notes about the text on the chart to answer the question: *What sequence of events caused the colonists to declare independence from Britain?*

Oscar

Event
The British government passed the Stamp Act. Colonists thought the new tax was unfair.

Event
British soldiers killed colonists in the Boston Massacre in 1770.

Event
In 1775, British troops attacked militias near Boston.

Event
In 1776, Congress approved the Declaration of Independence.

Write About the Text I used notes from my chart to write about the events that caused colonists to declare independence.

Student Model: *Informative Text*

A sequence of events caused the colonies to declare independence from Britain. First, the British government passed the Stamp Act. The colonists thought the new tax was unfair. They had protests. Next, British soldiers killed colonists in the Boston Massacre in 1770. Then in 1775, British troops attacked militias near Boston. These events caused Congress to approve the Declaration of Independence in 1776.

TALK ABOUT IT

Text Evidence

Draw a box around a sentence that comes from the notes. Did Oscar use the information in sequence?

Grammar

Circle a past tense verb. Why did Oscar use past tense verbs to write the paragraph?

Connect Ideas

Underline the sentences that tell how colonists reacted to the new tax. How can you use the word *so* to connect the sentences?

Your Turn

What is the author's point of view of the British? Use text evidence in your writing.

>> *Go Digital!*
Write your response online. Use your editing checklist.

TALK ABOUT IT

Essential Question
What can you do to get the information you need?

>> *Go Digital*

16

Where is the girl? What does she see? How do people get information? Write how people get information in the chart.

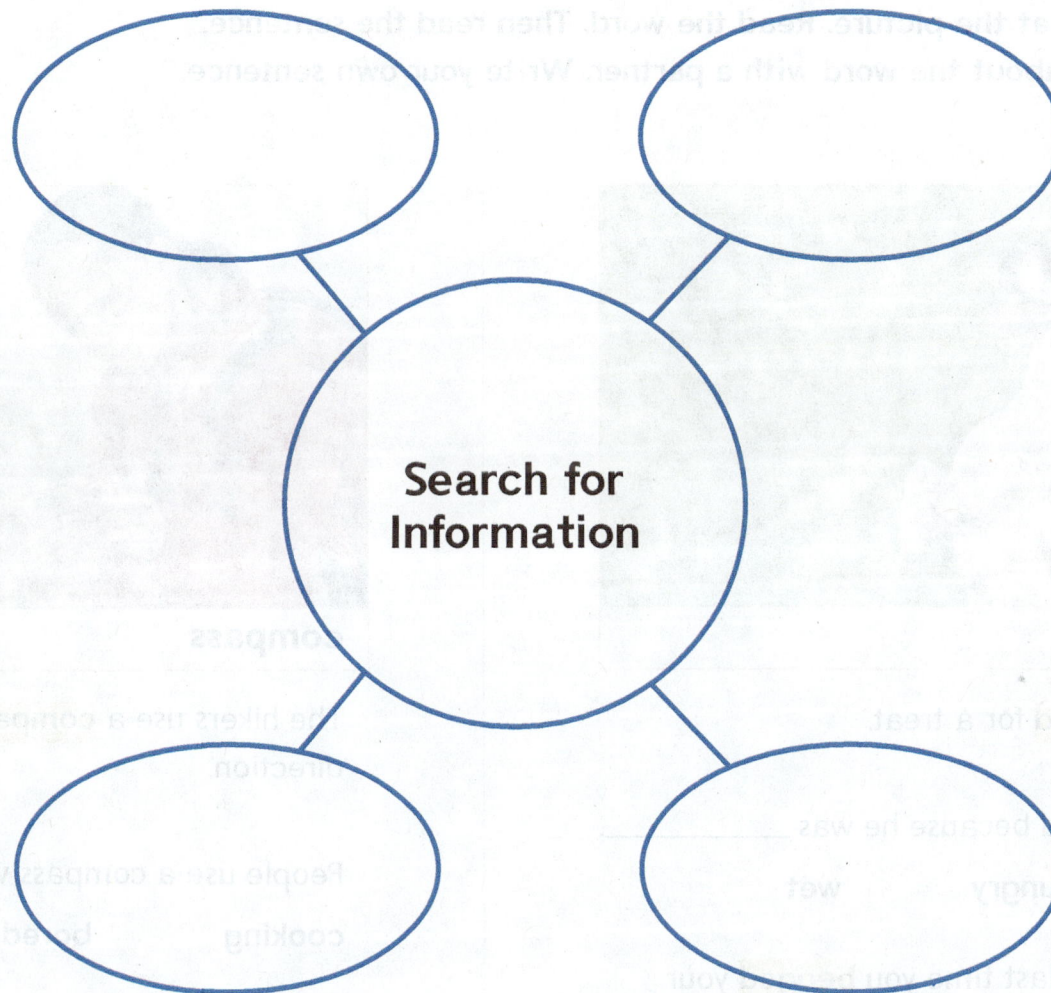

Search for Information

Discuss how the girl can get information. Use words from the chart. Complete these sentences.

The girl can read _____.

She can search the _____. She can talk to _____.

COLLABORATE Look at the picture. Read the word. Then read the sentence. Talk about the word with a partner. Write your own sentence.

begged

The dog **begged** for a treat.

The dog begged because he was _____.

tired   **hungry**   **wet**

When was the last time you **begged** your parents for something?

I begged for_____

_____.

compass

The hikers use a **compass** to find the direction.

People use a compass when they are _____.

cooking   **bored**   **lost**

What does a **compass** show you?

A compass shows me _____

_____.

Words and Phrases: *left* and *left behind*

One meaning of the word *left* is "remaining."

How many eggs are left?

There is one egg **left**.

The phrase *left behind* means "went away without taking."

What did the people do?

The people **left behind** their trash.

COLLABORATE Talk with a partner. Look at the pictures. Read the sentences. Write the word that completes each sentence.

There are two oranges _____.

    left   **left behind**

Someone _____ a jacket.

    left   **left behind**

Mark Steinmetz/McGraw-Hill Education; peterhowell/iStock/360/Getty Images; sola deo gloria/Moment Open/Getty Images; Ingram Publishing

19

A Modern Cinderella

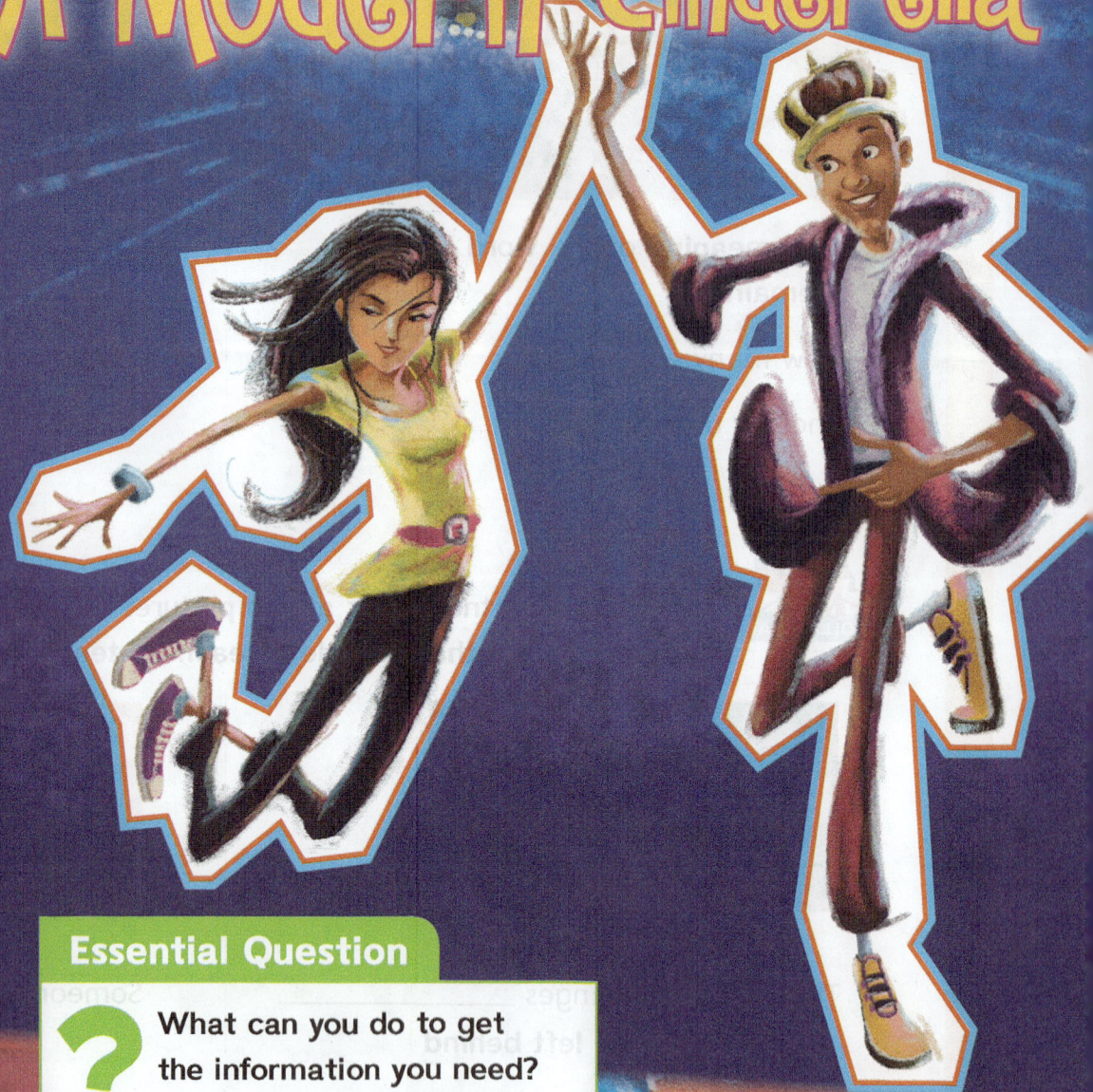

COLLABORATE

1 Talk About It

Look at the picture. Read the title. Discuss what you see. Use these words.

dancing   floor   sneaker together

Write about what you see.

This story is about _____

_____.

What are the boy and girl doing?

They are _____

_____.

Where are the boy and the girl?

They are on the dance _____

_____

Take notes as you read the story.

Essential Question

? **What can you do to get the information you need?**

Read how a Prince gets information about a girl.

Once upon a time, Prince lived at the Royal Palace with his mother, the Queen. He had a TV show called *Dancing with the Prince.* Prince taped the TV show at the Royal Palace. During one show, Prince danced with a lovely young woman. He felt like he was floating on a cloud.

However, circumstances changed at midnight. As people applauded Prince and the woman, the woman's cell phone rang. She ran from the palace and left behind a purple sneaker.

The Prince yelled, "I must find her again!" He held the purple sneaker tightly in his hand. How should he search?

His mind raced like a galloping horse. After much consideration, he made a plan. First, he interviewed everyone at the show, but no one could help. Next, the Prince searched the Internet using the phrase "great dancer with purple shoes." No results came up. Finally, he put up posters of the sneaker on the kingdom's social network. Yet no one knew the owner.

The McGraw-Hill Companies, Inc./Peter Francis

Text Evidence

❶ Specific Vocabulary Ⓐ Ⓒ Ⓣ

The phrase *Once upon a time* means "in the past." Reread the second sentence. Circle the words that tell you about the time period. How far in the past is the story?

❷ Sentence Structure Ⓐ Ⓒ Ⓣ

Reread the second sentence in the second paragraph. What word tells that two events happened at the same time? Undeline the text.

Two events that happened are

_____

_____.

❸ Comprehension

Compare and Contrast

Reread the last paragraph. What three things did Prince do? Put a box around the text that tells you. How are the three things alike?

The three things are alike because

_____

_____

❶ Talk About It

Reread the second paragraph. What were the results of Prince's visits? Write about it.

The results of the visits were _____

_____.

❷ Comprehension
Compare and Contrast

Reread the second sentence in the third paragraph. What does the author compare Prince's heart to? Underline the text. Write about it.

Prince feels _____

_____.

❸ Specific Vocabulary Ⓐ Ⓒ Ⓣ

The word *reluctantly* means "doing something you don't want to do." What does the sister do reluctantly? Circle the text.

The Prince held in his hands the purple sneaker and a computer **compass**. He cried, "I will visit every house in the entire kingdom." Then, he hopped on an electric skateboard and began the search.

The Prince visited many homes throughout the kingdom. At the first house, the woman's foot was too large for the sneaker. At the second house, the woman's foot was too small. At every home, the purple sneaker was too small or too big for the woman's foot.

As the days passed, Prince grew sadder. His heart was a cell phone in need of recharging. Finally, there was one house left to visit. When Prince arrived, three women stood in front, ready to try on the purple sneaker. The sneaker didn't fit any of them.

The Prince asked, "Does anyone else live here?" The sisters looked angry. Finally, one sister rolled her eyes and reluctantly sent a text to her stepsister. Then, the stepsister came outside.

The McGraw-Hill Companies, Inc./Peter Francis

22

Prince held out the sneaker. "Please try this on," he said. The sneaker fit her foot perfectly!

"You're the dancer!" the Prince yelled. "Will you be my dance partner forever?"

The woman replied, "Thanks, but I can only be your partner tomorrow. I have a lot of plans."

The Prince **begged**, "Please, say yes! After all, this is a fairy tale. I want a happy ending."

The girl said. "Sorry, Prince. You'll just have to wait."

Prince sighed, "Okay, I can wait, but tell me your name."

"It's Cinderella," she replied. She wrote on a piece of paper. "Here's my number. Let's stay in touch. TTYLP."

The Prince looked confused.

"It means Talk To You Later, Prince," Cinderella explained.

"TTYLC," the Prince replied. He waved to Cinderella and rode away.

And they texted happily ever after.

Make Connections

? Talk about how the Prince got the information he needed. What did he do? **ESSENTIAL QUESTION**

Have you searched for something or someone? How did you search? **TEXT TO SELF**

1 Sentence Structure A C T

Reread the third paragraph. Cinderella says no to the Prince. Underline the text that tells you. What reason does she give?

Cinderella says no because _____

_____.

2 Specific Vocabulary

The phrase *stay in touch* means to talk or write to someone. How does Cinderella want to stay in touch with the Prince? Circle the text.

Cinderella will stay in touch by

_____.

COLLABORATE

3 Talk About It

Does Cinderella like the Prince? Discuss. Then write your answer.

I think Cinderella _____

the Prince because _____

_____.

23

Respond to the Text

Partner Discussion Work with a partner. Read the questions about "A Modern Cinderella." Show where you found text evidence. Write the page numbers. Then discuss what you read.

How did the Prince meet the woman with the purple sneaker?

Prince met the woman at _____.

Prince thought the woman was _____

_____

Text Evidence 🔍

Page(s): _____

Page(s): _____

What did the Prince do to find the woman?

Prince visited _____ in his kingdom.

At each house, Prince asked the woman to _____, but

the purple sneaker _____.

Finally, at the last house Prince found _____

_____

Cinderella told Prince _____.

Text Evidence 🔍

Page(s): _____

Page(s): _____

Page(s): _____

Page(s): _____

Group Discussion Present your answers to the group. Cite text evidence for your ideas. Listen to and discuss the group's opinions.

Write Work with a partner. Look at your notes about "A Modern Cinderella." Write your answer to the Essential Question. Use text evidence to support your answer. Use vocabulary words in your writing.

How did the Prince find Cinderella?

The Prince made a plan to _____.

The Prince visited all the _____.

He asked the woman in each house to _____.

Finally, he found Cinderella at _____.

Cinderella told Prince _____.

They decided to _____.

Share Writing Present your writing to the class. Discuss their opinions. Talk about their ideas. Explain why you agree or disagree with their ideas. You can say:

I agree with _____.

I do not agree because _____.

Write to Sources

Kara

Take Notes About the Text I took notes on the chart to answer the question: *What did Cinderella and the mysterious caller talk about during the phone call?*

pages 20–23

Text Clue	Conclusion
At midnight Cinderella's cell phone rang.	The caller phones Cinderella to tell her something.
She ran from the palace.	Cinderella needed to go somewhere quickly.
She left behind a purple sneaker.	She ran so fast, she forgot her sneaker.

Write About the Text I used my notes from my chart to write a dialogue between Cinderella and the caller.

Cinderella heard the cell phone ring. She answered the phone.

Cinderella asked, "Hello. Why did you call me?"

The caller said, "It's midnight! Remember that we have a meeting."

Cinderella said, "OK. I'm leaving right now. I will run so the Prince doesn't see me."

The caller yelled, "Hurry!"

Cinderella ran from the palace. She ran very fast. She left behind one purple sneaker.

TALK ABOUT IT

COLLABORATE

Text Evidence

Draw a box around a sentence that comes from the notes. Is the information from a text clue or a conclusion?

Grammar

Circle a future-tense verb. Why did Kara use a future-tense verb?

Condense Ideas

Underline the two sentences that tell about how Cinderella runs. How can you combine the sentences into one detailed sentence?

Your Turn

COLLABORATE

Add an event to the story. Tell what the Prince said at the beginning of his TV show. Use text evidence in your writing.

>> Go Digital!
Write your response online. Use your editing checklist.

27

? **Essential Question**

How do we investigate questions about nature?

>> *Go Digital*

What do you see when you look closely at a grasshopper? What can you see when you investigate nature? Write what you see in the chart.

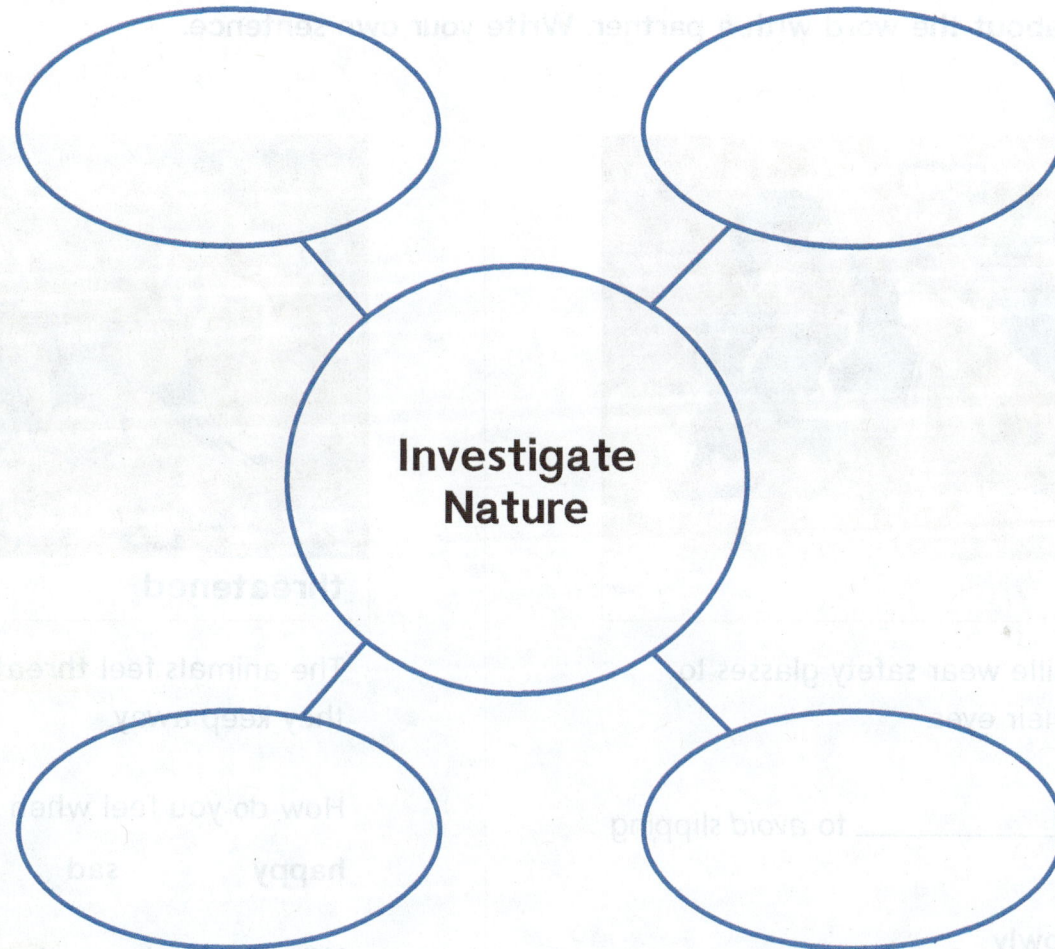

Investigate
Nature

Discuss what you can see when you investigate nature. Use words from the chart. You can say:

When I look closely, the grasshopper has _____.

When I investigate nature, I can see _____.

More Vocabulary

COLLABORATE Look at the picture. Read the word. Then read the sentence.
Talk about the word with a partner. Write your own sentence.

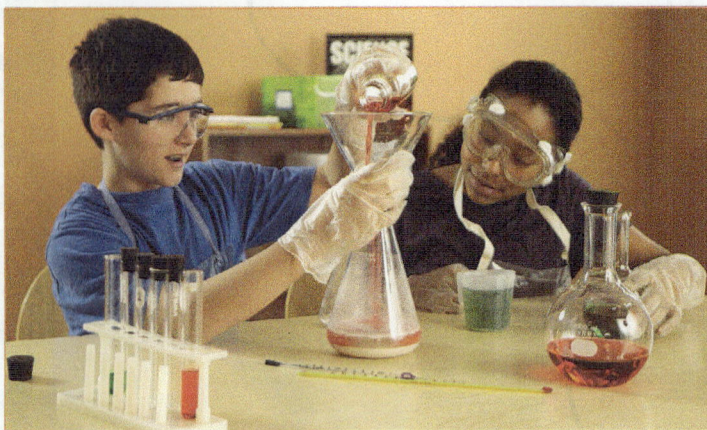

avoid

Justin and Camille wear safety glasses to **avoid** hurting their eyes.

Sheila walks _____ to *avoid* slipping

on the ice.
quickly   **slowly**

What safety equipment do you wear to avoid getting hurt?

To avoid getting hurt, I wear _____.

threatened

The animals feel **threatened** by the lion, so they keep away.

How do you feel when you are *threatened*?

happy   **sad**   **scared**

What animals are threatened by snakes?

_____ are *threatened*

by snakes.

Words and Phrases: *found in* and *interested in*

The phrase *found in* means "seen" or "discovered."

Where were the owls?

The owls were **found in** the barn.

The phrase *interested in* means "wanting to know or learn about."

What game is Abdul interested in?

Abdul is **interested in** chess.

COLLABORATE Talk with a partner. Look at the pictures. Read the sentences. Write the word that completes each sentence.

The children are _____ fishing.

found in   interested in

The fossils were _____ the forest.

found in   interested in

COLLABORATE

❶ Talk About It

Look at the illustrations. Read the title. Discuss what you see. Use these words.

plants   flowers   study   name

What does the title tell you?

This text is about _____

_____

_____.

What did E. Lucy Braun study? Explain your answer.

I think she studied _____

_____

because _____

_____

_____.

Take notes as you read the text.

Growing in Place

The Story of
E. Lucy Braun

iris

Essential Question

?

How do we investigate questions about nature?

Read about how Lucy Braun's classification of plants helps scientists.

Lucy's Childhood

Emma Lucy Braun was born in 1889 in Cincinnati, Ohio. She had the same first name as her mother. So she used her middle name, Lucy, to <mark>avoid</mark> confusion. Naming things correctly became an important part of her work on plants.

From a young age, Lucy was interested in plants. Her family often took walks in the woods. Lucy enjoyed looking at the plants and wildflowers.

Lucy's mother taught Lucy to observe the plants and identify them. Lucy examined the shape and the number of leaves on a stem. Then, Lucy wrote about what she saw and drew the plants. Soon, she knew enough to compare and contrast many plants.

Lucy and her mother had a collection of dried plants, or a herbarium. First, they gathered leaves and flowers. Then they pressed them between sheets of paper. Lucy became more interested in botany, the study of plants. In high school, she started her own herbarium. She added plants to it all her life.

pink redstem filagrees

(bkgd) RoseAnn Hayes; (inset) Library of Congress - Archive of Folk Culture (CRF-MH-C020-02)

1 **Sentence Structure** Ⓐ Ⓒ Ⓣ

Reread the third sentence in the first paragraph. Why did Lucy use her middle name? Underline the text that tells you.

Lucy used her middle name

because _____

_____.

2 **Specific Vocabulary** Ⓐ Ⓒ Ⓣ

The word *observe* means "to watch carefully." Circle the text that tells how Lucy observed the plants.

When you observe something, you

_____

_____

3 **Comprehension**
Sequence

Reread the fourth paragraph. How did Lucy get her own herbarium?

First, Lucy and her mother _____

_____.

Then Lucy _____

_____.

1 Sentence Structure Ⓐ Ⓒ Ⓣ

Reread the third sentence. What subjects did Lucy study? Circle the text that tells you. What is geology?

Geology is _____

_____ .

2 Specific Vocabulary Ⓐ Ⓒ Ⓣ

Something that happens *over time* means it happened during a long period of time. What happened over time? Underline the text that tells you.

COLLABORATE

3 Talk About It

Reread the third paragraph. How do you know Lucy was very interested in botany?

I know Lucy was interested in

botany because _____

_____

_____ .

Lucy Braun's Snakeroot: This plant grows in Kentucky and Tennessee.

iris

robin's egg

nest

Scientists make sketches to learn to see details.

Growing Up

Lucy and her sister Annette studied at the University of Cincinnati. Annette studied insects to become an entomologist. Lucy studied geology, or the study of rocks and minerals, and botany, too.

Lucy also was interested in ecology, which studies how living things interact with environments. Some ecologists helped Lucy test an important theory, or idea. Lucy believed that plants moved from one place to another over time. She mapped how plants had moved since the Ice Age.

Collecting Information

In 1917, Lucy began to teach botany at the University of Cincinnati. Lucy and Annette lived together and they studied science at home, too. Lucy took care of an indoor and outdoor garden. Annette studied the moths that fluttered outside.

Lucy collected plants from around the country. She photographed many of them. Many people enjoyed Lucy's color photographs, lectures, and slide shows.

A Life of Science

Later in her life, Lucy wrote many field guides. Field guides are books that identify plants. In 1950, Lucy published her most important guide. The guide described the forest plants found in the eastern United States. Scientists still use it.

Today, Lucy has a few plants named after her. One plant is called Lucy Braun's snakeroot. The plant is **threatened**. Lucy's work helps scientists save rare plants.

Lucy Braun lived to be 81 years old. As a botanist, Lucy collected nearly 12,000 plants. Her herbarium is in the Smithsonian Institution in Washington, D.C. Visitors can see the plants she collected all her life.

Make Connections

? Talk about how Lucy's mother helped Lucy study plants. **ESSENTIAL QUESTION**

Tell about a collection that you have. How do you organize the collection? **TEXT TO SELF**

(bkgd) RoseAnn Hayes; (inset) J.S. Peterson/USDA

Plant Identification

Become a botanist! Follow the steps to identify plants in your area.

Materials: magnifying glass, field guide

1. Identify the places where plants grow.

2. Identify the plants as evergreen or broad leaf.

3. Draw or photograph the leaf. Record the shape and other details.

4. Observe how the leaves appear on the stem.

5. Look at the plants in the field guide. Find a match.

Text Evidence

1 **Specific Vocabulary** Ⓐ Ⓒ Ⓣ

The word *rare* means "something you don't see or find often." What plant is rare? Underline the text.

2 **Comprehension Sequence**

Reread the first paragraph. Circle the signal words. What do the signal words describe?

The signal words _____

_____ tell about when Lucy

was _____.

COLLABORATE

3 **Talk About It**

How does Lucy Braun's work help scientists and people today?

Scientists use Lucy's work to _____

_____.

People can see _____

_____.

Respond to the Text

Partner Discussion Work with a partner. Read the questions about "Growing in Place." Show where you found text evidence. Write the page numbers. Then discuss what you learned.

How did Lucy Braun become interested in plants as a child?

Text Evidence 🔍

With her family, Lucy _____.   Page(s): _____

Lucy's mother taught Lucy to tell the plants apart by _____   Page(s): _____

_____.

They had a collection of _____.   Page(s): _____

How did Lucy Braun study plants later in life?

Text Evidence 🔍

In college, Lucy tested a theory about _____   Page(s): _____

_____.

In college, Lucy mapped _____.   Page(s): _____

At home, Lucy studied _____ and collected _____.   Page(s): _____

Later in life, Lucy wrote _____   Page(s): _____

Group Discussion Present your answers to the group. Cite text evidence for your ideas. Listen to and discuss the group's opinions.

Write Work with a partner. Look at your notes about "Growing in Place." Write your answer to the Essential Question. Use text evidence to support your answer. Use vocabulary words in your writing.

How did Lucy Braun investigate plants?

When Lucy was young, she learned to _____

_____ .

In college, Lucy continued to study about plants. She _____

_____ .

Later in life, Lucy _____

_____ .

Share Writing Present your writing to the class. Discuss their opinions. Talk about their ideas. Explain why you agree or disagree with their ideas. You can say:

I agree with _____ .

I do not agree because _____ .

Write to Sources

pages 32–35

Take Notes About the Text I took notes about the text on the chart to answer the question: *How does the Plant Identification sidebar help support the information in the text?*

Darius

Detail

Step 2 tells to identify plants using leaves. Lucy learned to examine the shape of the leaves.

Topic

The Plant Identification sidebar supports the information in the text.

Detail

Step 3 tells to draw or photograph the leaves and record details. Lucy learned to write about and draw the plants.

Detail

Step 5 tells to match the plant in the field guide. Lucy wrote field guides.

Write About the Text I used notes from my chart to write about how the sidebar supports the information in the text.

Student Model: *Informative Text*

The Plant Identification sidebar supports the information about the work Lucy Braun did. For example, step 2 in the sidebar tells to identify plants using the leaves. Lucy examined the shape of the leaves in the woods. Step 3 tells to draw or photograph the leaves. Lucy wrote about the plants. She drew the plants. Step 5 tells to match the plant from a field guide. Lucy wrote field guides. The steps support the things Lucy did for her work with plants.

TALK ABOUT IT

COLLABORATE

Text Evidence

Draw a box around a sentence that comes from the notes. Does the sentence provide detail for the topic?

Grammar

Circle a proper noun. How is a proper noun different from a regular noun?

Connect Ideas

Underline the sentences that describe a step from the sidebar and what Lucy did. How can you use the word *and* to connect the sentences?

Your Turn

COLLABORATE

Who or what helped Lucy to become a scientist? Use text evidence in your writing.

>> Go Digital!
Write your response online. Use your editing checklist.

? Essential Question

When has a plan helped you accomplish a task?

>> *Go Digital*

What is the man in the photograph doing? How can a plan help people do things? Describe how making a plan helps you.

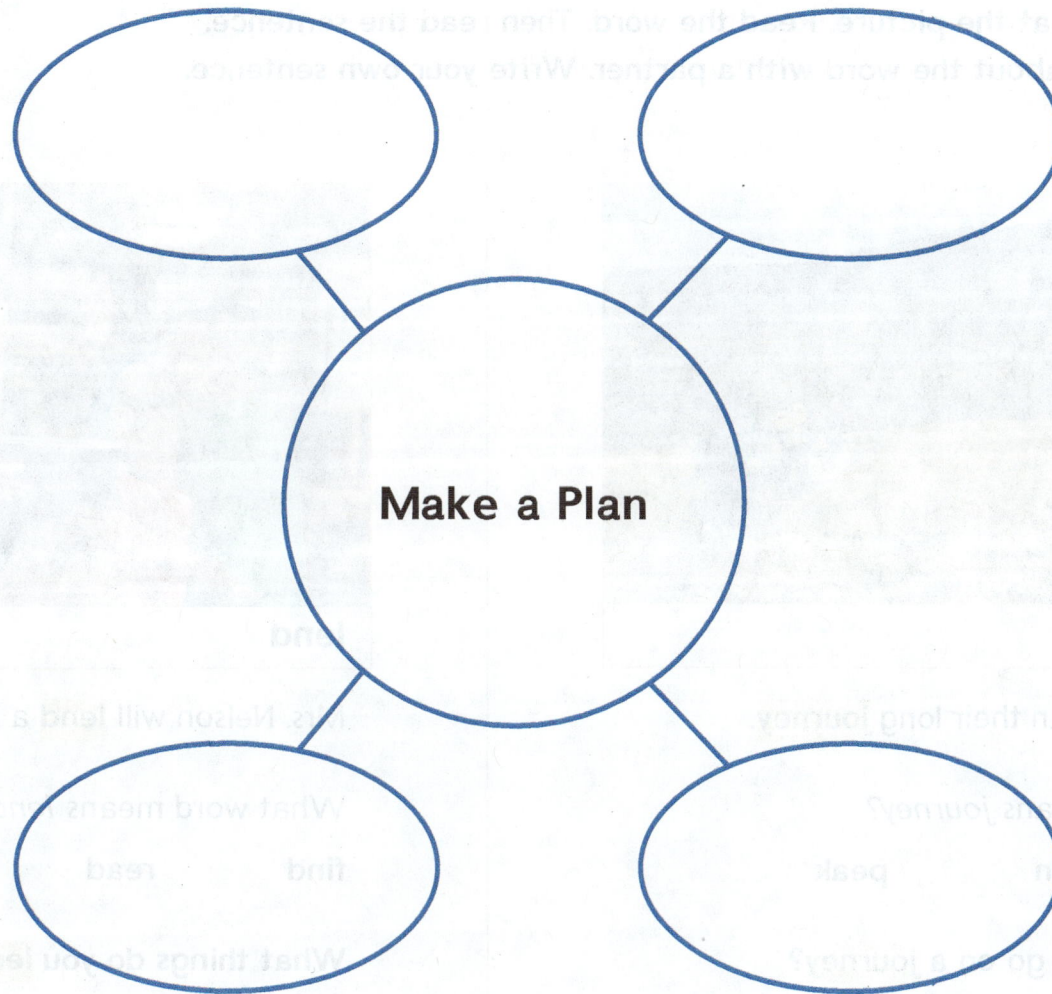

```
          (          )              (          )
           \                         /
            \                       /
             \                     /
              \                   /
               (                 )
              (                   )
             (                     )
            (      Make a Plan      )
             (                     )
              (                   )
               (                 )
              /                   \
             /                     \
            /                       \
       (         )              (         )
```

Discuss how a plan helps people do things. Use words from the chart. Complete the sentences.

A plan is helpful for _____ because

_____.

More Vocabulary

Look at the picture. Read the word. Then read the sentence.
Talk about the word with a partner. Write your own sentence.

journey

The hikers began their long <mark>journey</mark>.

What word means *journey*?

trip   run   peak

Where did you go on a <mark>journey</mark>?

I went to _____.

on my journey.

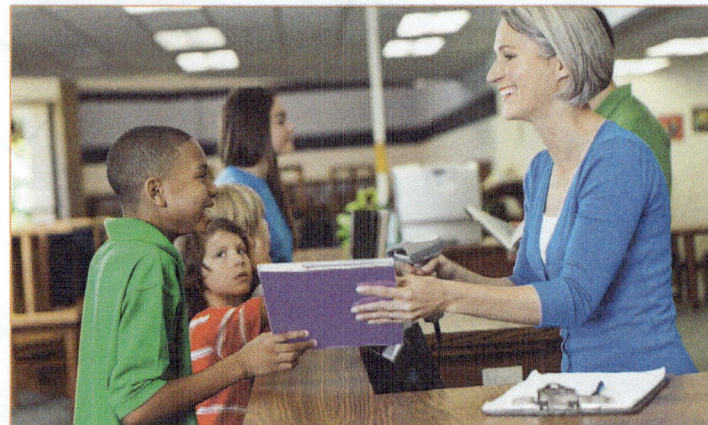

lend

Mrs. Nelson will <mark>lend</mark> a book to John.

What word means *lend*?

find   read   loan

What things do you <mark>lend</mark> to a friend?

I lend _____

to a friend.

Words and Phrases: *arrived at* and *arrived home*

The word *arrived at* means "reached a place."

Where did the plane go?

The plane **arrived at** the airport.

The words *arrived home* mean "reached my home."

When did the students get home?

They **arrived home** in the afternoon.

COLLABORATE

Talk with a partner. Look at the pictures. Read the sentences. Write the word or phrase that completes each sentence.

The students _____ school in the morning.

arrived at   arrived home

The father _____ after shopping for groceries.

arrived at   arrived home

COLLABORATE

1 Talk About It

Look at the illustration. Read the title. Discuss what you see. Use these words.

palace   brocade   mountain ocean

Write about what you see.

What is the folktale about?

This folktale is about _____

_____

_____.

Who kind of place do you see?

The place is _____

_____

_____.

Take notes as you read the story.

The Magical Lost Brocade

Essential Question

? **When has a plan helped you accomplish a task?**

Read about how a young man finds a lost brocade.

Long ago, in China, a poor woman and her son, Ping, lived in a hut. The woman weaved brocade hangings, and Ping sold them. The woman wished for a better home, but that was impossible. Instead, she weaved a brocade of a magnificent house with gardens. It took three years to complete, but it was her best work. One day, a great wind carried the brocade away! The woman was very sad. So Ping promised to bring back the brocade and left home.

Ping walked for three days **until** he saw a bearded man sitting in front of a stone house. "I'm searching for my mother's brocade," Ping said.

"There is a brocade in a palace far away. I'll explain how to get there and **lend** you my horse," the man said. Ping bowed to thank him.

The man explained to Ping, "First, you must ride through Fire Valley. You must ride through it without saying a word or you'll burn! Then, You must cross Ice Ocean. You must cross it without shivering or the sea will swallow you up! Finally, you must ride up the Mountain of the Sun. The palace sits on top of the mountain, and the brocade is in the palace."

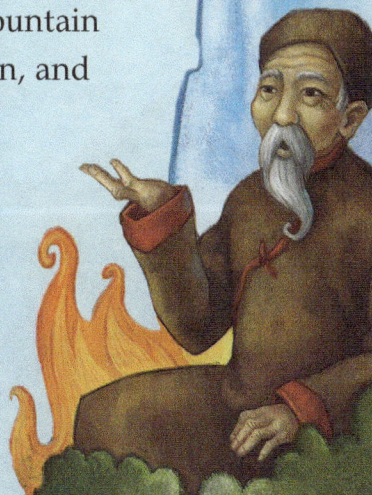

Shawna Tenney

1 Sentence Structure **A C T**

Reread the fifth sentence. The sentence has two parts. In both parts, the word *it* refers to the same thing. Circle the text that *it* refers to. What does the sentence tell you about *it*?

The sentence tells that *it* _____

_____.

2 Specific Vocabulary **A C T**

The word *until* tells you that a new event happened and the previous event stopped. What new event happened? Underline the text.

3 Comprehension

Reread the last paragraph. What three tasks did the bearded man give Ping? Put a box around the text that tells you.

The three tasks Ping had to do

were _____,

_____, and

_____.

1 Sentence Structure Ⓐ Ⓒ Ⓣ

Reread the fourth sentence. Circle the verbs. Underline the subjects. Are the two events happening at the same time? Explain.

The two events are happening _____

_____.

The word _____ tells me.

2 Specific Vocabulary Ⓐ Ⓒ Ⓣ

Reached means "arrived at." How did Ping reach the top of the mountain? Use the word *reached*.

Ping _____

_____

COLLABORATE

3 Talk About It

Reread the last paragraph. Discuss what happened to the brocade.

Princess Ling took the brocade

because _____.

"It sounds like a very difficult journey," said Ping. He got on the horse and traveled. After three days, Ping arrived at Fire Valley. As Ping rode through the valley, he felt the hot flames from the fire. The heat brought tears to his eyes, but he said nothing.

When Ping reached the other side of the Fire Valley, he saw the Ice Ocean. Ping rode into the icy waters, but he didn't shiver until they crossed the sea safely.

Next, Ping saw the Mountain of the Sun and rode to the top. The mountain was very steep, so he held tightly to the reins. Finally, he reached the palace at the top of the mountain.

A lovely princess welcomed him. She said, "I'm Princess Ling. I thought your mother's brocade was beautiful, so I sent a great wind to get it. I copied the brocade, so please take it home."

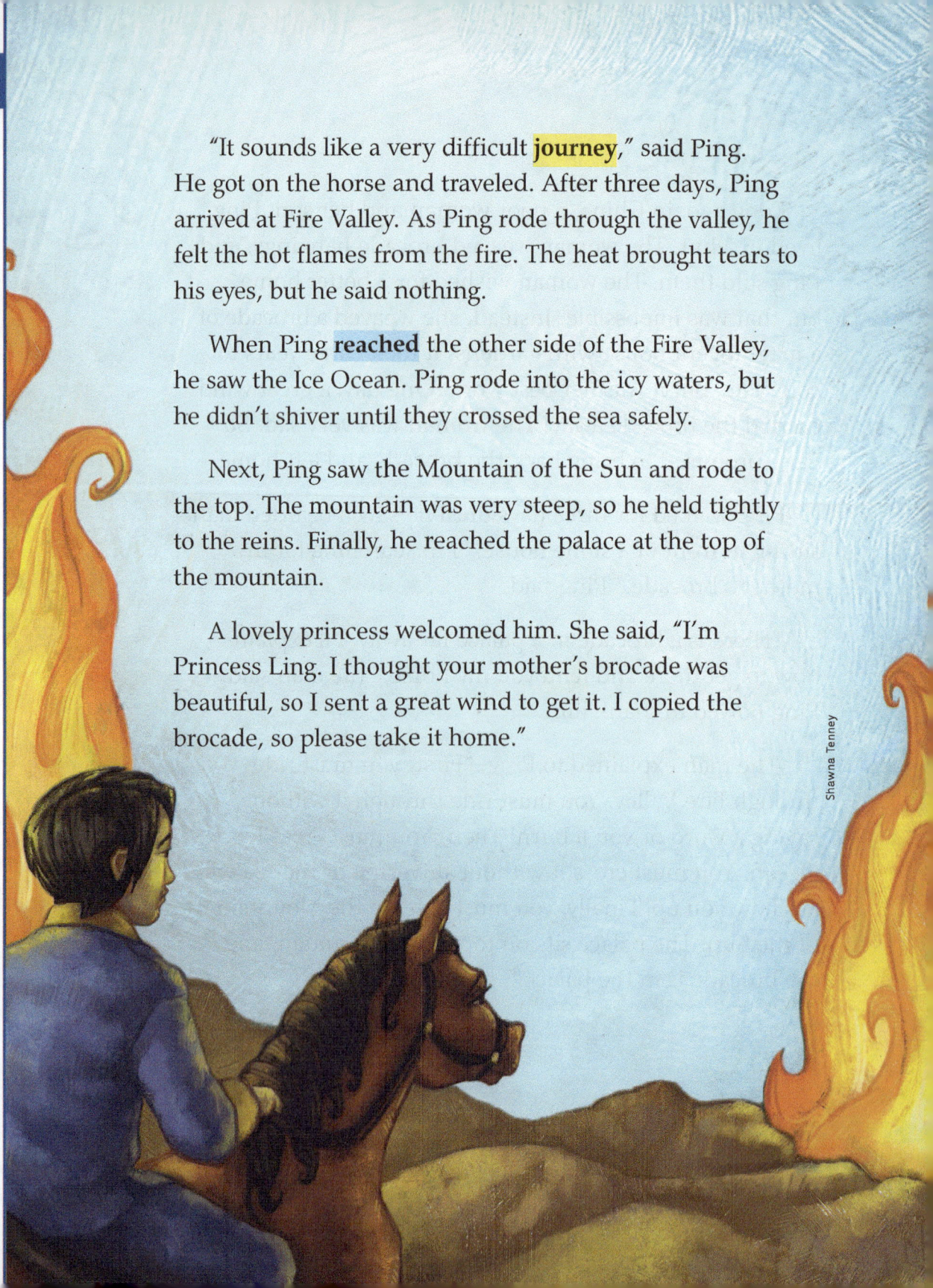

Shawna Tenney

"Thank you," said Ping. He thought the princess was beautiful and hoped he could see her again. Ping detected a quick smile on her face as they said good-bye.

Ping put the brocade inside his jacket and got on the horse. First, he rode down the Mountain of the Sun. Next, he rode across the Ice Ocean, without shivering once. Then, he rode across Fire Valley, without making a sound. Finally, he arrived at the home of the bearded man. Ping thanked the man and returned the horse.

Three days later Ping arrived home and gave the brocade to his mother. She **cried tears of joy**. They unrolled the brocade together. Suddenly, their hut changed into the magnificent house and gardens from the brocade. Princess Ling appeared, too! Ping and the princess got married. They lived happily with Ping's mother in their beautiful home and gardens!

Make Connections

? Talk about Ping's plan. How did following the plan help Ping find the lost brocade? ESSENTIAL QUESTION

When have you followed a plan to accomplish a task? TEXT TO SELF

Text Evidence 🔍

❶ Sentence Structure 🅐🅒🅣

Reread the third sentence in the second paragraph. What did Ping do? Circle the text. What did Ping *not* do? Underline the text.

Ping _____, but

he did not _____.

❷ Specific Vocabulary 🅐🅒🅣

The phrase *cried tears of joy* means "cried because of happiness." Who cried? Why was the person happy? Underline the text.

_____ cried tears of joy

because _____.

❸ Comprehension
Theme

Reread the last paragraph. Did Ping keep the promise to his mother? Put a box around the text that tells you. How did a plan help Ping?

The plan helped Ping because

_____.

Respond to the Text

Partner Discussion Work with a partner. Read the questions about "The Magical Lost Brocade." Show where you found text evidence. Write the page numbers. Then discuss what you read.

What plan does Ping follow to reach the palace?

First, Ping rides _____.

Text Evidence 🔍

Page(s): _____

Then, Ping crosses _____.

Page(s): _____

Finally, Ping rides up _____.

Page(s): _____

How did following the plan help Ping?

On the mountain, Ping meets _____.

Text Evidence 🔍

Page(s): _____

Princess Ling tells Ping _____.

Page(s): _____

When Ping brings the brocade home, _____
_____.

Page(s): _____

Group Discussion Present your answers to the group. Cite text evidence for your ideas. Listen to and discuss the group's opinions.

Write Work with a partner. Look at your notes about "The Magical Lost Brocade." Write your answer to the Essential Question. Use text evidence to support your answer. Use vocabulary words in your writing.

How does a plan help Ping find the lost brocade?

In the story, Ping needs to _____.

The bearded man tells Ping _____.

Ping follows the plan by _____

_____.

The plan helps Ping because _____

_____.

Share Writing Present your writing to the class. Discuss their opinions. Talk about their ideas. Explain why you agree or disagree with their ideas. You can say:

I agree with _____.

I do not agree because _____.

Write to Sources

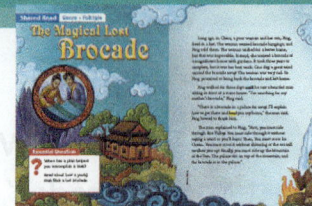

Take Notes About the Text I took notes about the text on the chart to answer the question: *What event could be added to show how Princess Ling gets to Ping's house?*

Callie

Text Clue	**Conclusion**
The princess lives in a palace. To get to the palace, Ping crossed Fire Valley, rode through Ice Ocean, and climbed the Mountain of the Sun.	The princess lives far away from Ping's home. It is difficult to travel.
Text Clue	**Conclusion**
The princess sent a great wind to get the brocade from Ping's house.	The princess has the power to use wind to get things for her.
Text Clue	**Conclusion**
Ping and his mother unrolled the brocade and the princess appeared.	The princess traveled by wind to get to Ping's house. She got inside the brocade. She appeared when Ping and his mother unrolled the brocade.

Write About the Text I used notes from my chart to write about how Princess Ling gets to Ping's house.

Student Model: *Narrative Text*

Princess Ling lived in a palace. The palace was far away from Ping's home. However, Princess Ling had the power to use wind to help her. Princess Ling decided to use wind to help her travel to Ping's home. First, she had the wind carry her to Ping's house. Next, she waited until Ping arrived. Then, she got inside the brocade. Finally, Ping and his mother unrolled the brocade. The princess appeared.

TALK ABOUT IT

COLLABORATE

Text Evidence
Draw a box around a sentence that comes from the notes. Is the information from a text clue or conclusion?

Grammar
Circle a possessive noun. What belongs to Ping?

Connect Ideas
Underline the two sentences that tell about unrolling the brocade. How can you use the word *when* to connect the sentences?

Your Turn

COLLABORATE

Write about another place that Ping travels through before the Ice Ocean. Use text evidence in your writing.

>> Go Digital!
Write your response online. Use your editing checklist.

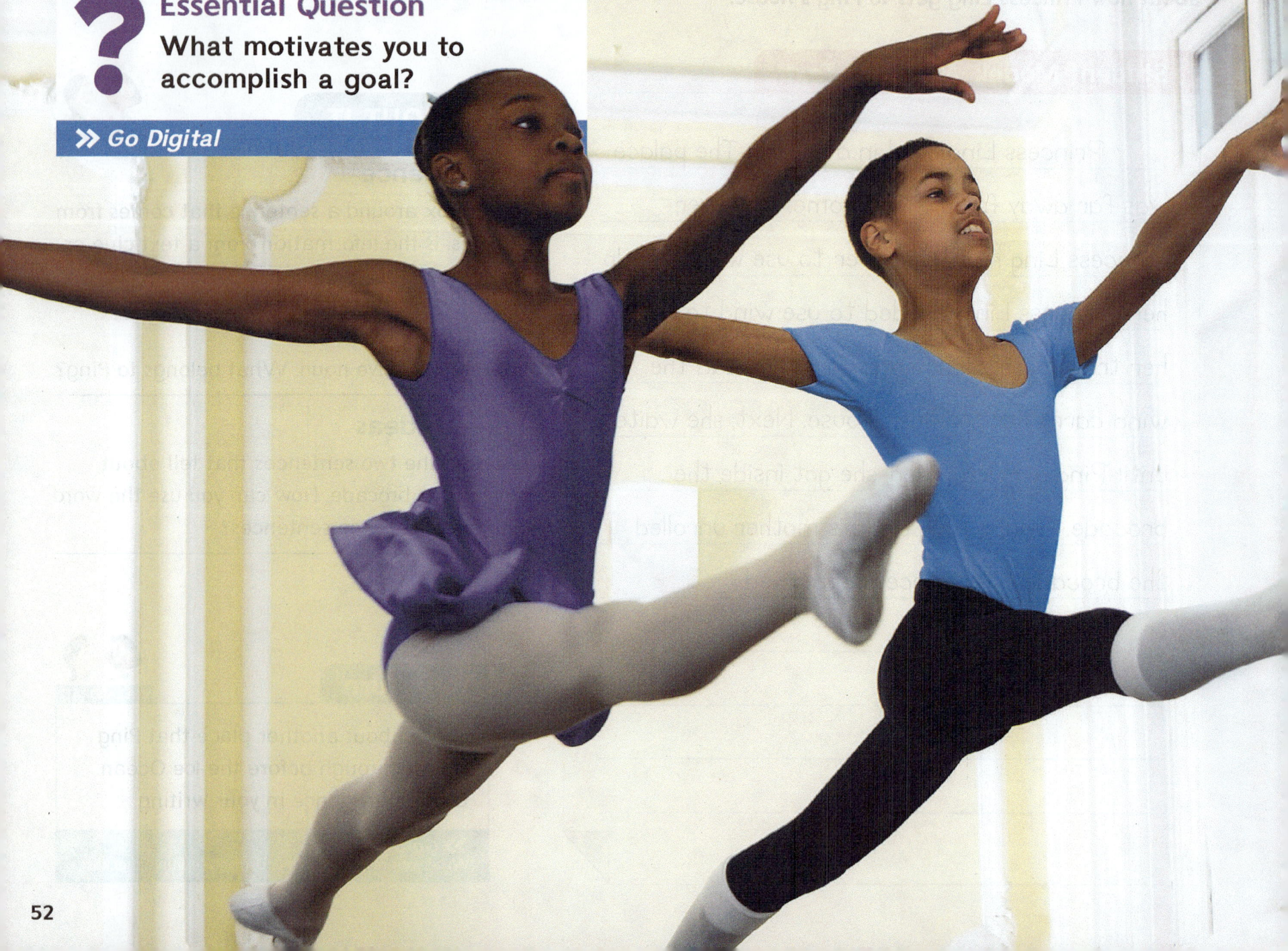

? Essential Question

What motivates you to accomplish a goal?

» *Go Digital*

What goal do the boy and girl in the photograph have? How can they accomplish, or reach, their goal? How do people reach their goals? Describe what they need to do in the chart.

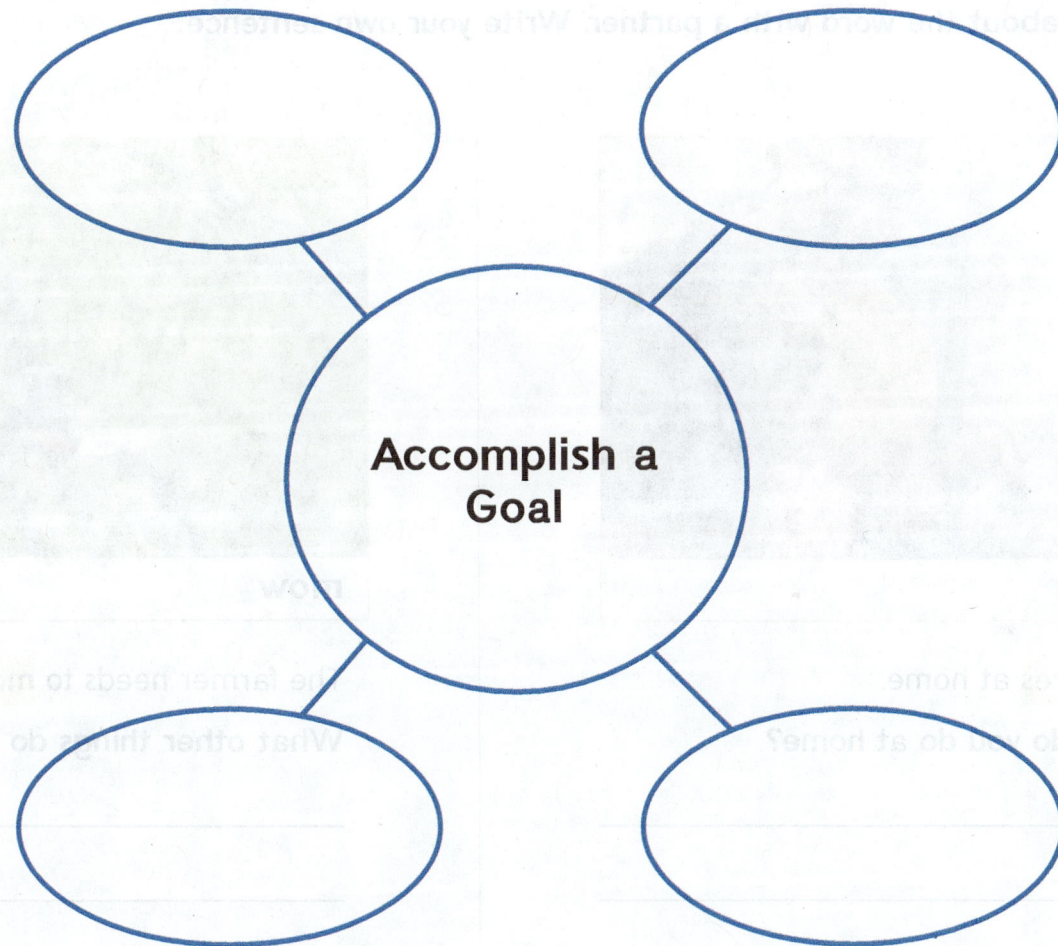

Accomplish a Goal

Discuss how people reach their goals. Use the words from the chart. Complete the sentence:

People need to _____

_____ to accomplish a goal.

More Vocabulary

Look at the picture. Read the word. Then read the sentence.
Talk about the word with a partner. Write your own sentence.

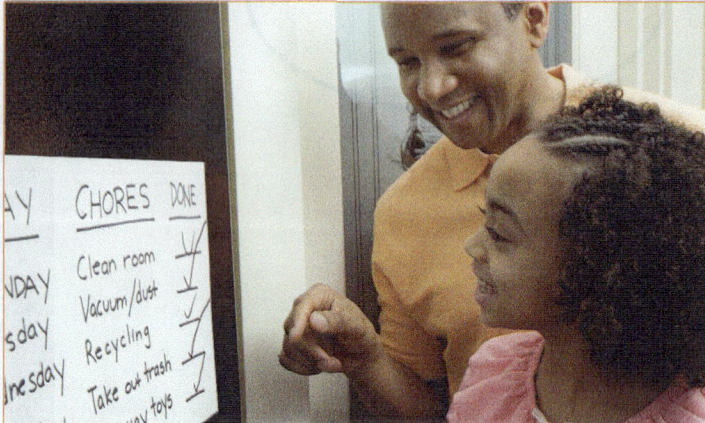

chores

Erika does **chores** at home.

What chores do you do at home?

_____

_____

_____

mow

The farmer needs to **mow** the field.

What other things do people mow?

_____

_____

_____

Poetry Terms

rhyme

Words that **rhyme** end in the same sound.

Jack has a pretty *flower*.
He plants it in a pot.
Then comes a rain *shower*.
The flower grows and grows.

The words *flower* and *shower* rhyme.

narrative

A **narrative** poem tells a story. It has characters and dialogues. Sometimes it has words that rhyme.

Mike will *mow* a lawn. But before the neighbors *know*, Mike is *done*.
Mike says "Goodbye, I must be *gone*."
The neighbors respond, "Thank you!"

This poem has a character and a dialogue. The words *mow* and *know* and *done* and *gone* rhyme.

COLLABORATE

Work with a partner. Make up a rhyme. Use the words below. Say it together.

mop   shop   drop

We buy flowers in the

_____.

We like to watch the

petals _____.

We clean them up

with a _____.

A Simple Plan

1 Specific Vocabulary Ⓐ Ⓒ Ⓣ

Reread line 2. The word *plot* means "a plan." What is Jack's plot? Circle the text. Why is the plot simple? Support your opinion.

The plot is simple because _____

_____

_____

COLLABORATE

2 Talk About It

Reread lines 3–8. What things can Jack do to "change the world"? Underline the text.

To change the world, Jack can

_____.

3 Literary Element
Rhyme

Reread lines 14–17. Circle the word that rhymes with *about*.

Each morning when Jack rises,
He schemes a simple plot:
"I think I'll change the world," says he,
"A little, not a lot."
For neighbors he might mow a lawn
Before they know he's done it,
Or lead a soccer match at school,
And not care which team won it.
Some kids would laugh,
but Jack would smile
And look for more to do.
He'd walk your dog or tell a joke,
Or play a song for you.
Jack's brother John just didn't see
What Jack was all about.
John shuddered at Jack's crazy ways,
But Jack had not one doubt.

(l) Peter Zander/Photolibrary/Getty Images; (r) Fancy/Alamy

Essential Question

?

What motivates you to accomplish a goal?

Read how a poet describes a goal and why it matters.

"Who wants to do another's chores?"
John asked. "What does it mean,
'I'll change the world?' You're wasting time.
What changes have you seen?"
"Little brother," Jack explained,
"I used to think like you.
I thought, 'Why bother?' and 'Who cares?'
I see you do that, too.
I'd see some grass not mowed, or else
Kids not getting along,
And in the park no games to play—
I'd wonder what was wrong.
And then I had to ask myself,
What was I waiting for?
The change can start with me, you see,
That key is in my door.
I've memorized a thousand names,
And everyone knows me.
What do *you* do?" John had to think.
And he began to see.
Now each morning when Jack rises,
He hears his brother plan:
"I think I'll change the world," says John,
"If I can't, then who can?"
— Peter Collier

Make Connections

? Talk about why the speaker wants to meet a goal.
ESSENTIAL QUESTION

Compare the speaker's feelings in the poem to the feelings
you have when you try to meet a goal. **TEXT TO SELF**

Text Evidence 🔍

❶ Literary Element
Narrative

Reread lines 1-5. Who are the
characters? Circle the names.

_____

❷ Specific Vocabulary 🅐🅒🅣

The phrases *Why bother?* and
Who cares? both mean "It doesn't
matter." What did Jack think didn't
matter? Underline the text.

Jack thought it didn't matter that

he tried to _____

_____

COLLABORATE
❸ Talk About It

Discuss what John learns from
Jack. Then write about it.

John learns that he can _____

_____

_____.

57

Respond to the Text

COLLABORATE

Partner Discussion Work with a partner. Read the questions about "A Simple Plan." Show where you found text evidence. Write the page numbers. Then discuss what you read.

What things does Jack do?	**Text Evidence**
Jack mows _____.	Page(s): _____
Jack leads _____.	Page(s): _____
Jack walks _____.	Page(s): _____

Why does Jack do these things?	**Text Evidence**
Jack wants to _____.	Page(s): _____
Jack thinks a change _____.	Page(s): _____
Jack convinces his brother to _____.	Page(s): _____

COLLABORATE

Group Discussion Present your answers to the group. Cite text evidence for your ideas. Listen to and discuss the group's opinions.

Write Work with a partner. Look at your notes about "A Simple Plan." Write your answer to the Essential Question. Use text evidence to support your answer. Use vocabulary words in your writing.

What motivates Jack to accomplish his simple plan?

Jack decided to change the world by _____

_____.

Jack made his decision because Jack believes _____.

Jack also helped his brother _____.

Now both brothers _____.

Share Writing Present your writing to the class. Discuss their opinions. Talk about their ideas. Explain why you agree or disagree with their ideas. You can say:

I agree with _____.

I do not agree because _____.

59

Pete

Take Notes About the Text I took notes about the text on the chart to answer the question: *How can you tell that "A Simple Plan" is a narrative poem?*

pages 56–57

Detail
The poem tells a story about Jack. Jack makes a plan to change the world.

Topic
The poem "A Simple Plan" is a narrative poem.

Detail
The poem has characters Jack and John.

Detail
The poem has dialogue between Jack and John.

Write About the Text I used notes from my chart to explain why "A Simple Plan" is a narrative poem.

Student Model: *Informative Text*

"A Simple Plan" is a narrative poem because it tells a story. The poem has characters and dialogue. First, the poem tells a story about Jack and John. Second, the poem describes the characters Jack and John. They are brothers. Jack helps John make a plan. Finally, the poem has a dialogue between Jack and John. John tells Jack about his plan to change the world. All of these reasons prove that "A Simple Plan" is a narrative poem.

TALK ABOUT IT

COLLABORATE

Text Evidence

Draw a box around the sentence that comes from the notes. Does the sentence describe the topic or details?

Grammar

Circle a prepositional phrase. What detail does the phrase tell?

Condense Ideas

Underline two sentences about the characters Jack and John. How can you condense the sentences?

Your Turn

COLLABORATE

Does the poet use rhyme in "A Simple Plan"? Use text evidence in your writing.

>> *Go Digital!*
Write your response online. Use your editing checklist.